Early and Late: Selected Poems

Early and Late

SELECTED POEMS

Donald Petersen

WINNER OF THE NEW CRITERION POETRY PRIZE

Ivan R. Dee

CHICAGO 2001

Library of Congress Cataloging-in-Publication Data:
Petersen, Donald.
   Early and late : selected poems / Donald Petersen.
      p. cm.
  ISBN 1-56663-397-4 (acid-free paper)
    I. Title.

PS3566.E76 E2 2001
811'.54—dc21
                                        2001028192

Contents

Early and Late: Selected Poems

Waiting for a Train at Cherbourg

Junior Year in France, 1948–1949

Customs is finished. Gulls in the low skies
Circle and circle. They seem to cry, Get wise—
The train is always late where the gull flies.

What now? To shuffle up and down the *quai*
In cloud-capped August, staring at the gray
Choppy Atlantic, passing the time of day.

Cliffs, chalky and sodden, glower in the gray
Distance, walling the bay. They seem to say
The harbor honky-tonks won't be it today.

Abelard accosted Héloïse. She wouldn't,
At first, consent. Villon, a later student,
Stole what he wanted. Nothing seemed imprudent.

Sentenced along with other students, banished
From grace and sanctuary, Villon vanished,
Though by his impious poems he rose replenished.

But Abelard got his. Disgraced forever,
He built a shack of sticks beside the river,
His students followed him in droves, however,

Set up their tents and huts beside his shack,
Disputing faith and logic, forth and back.
With Abelard, the gulls come screeching back. . . .

The *gare*, a drafty hangar, is. Where is
That blue-eyed Barnard girl? Bright gold her hair is.
She said she'd talk to me on the way to Paris.

The Cats of Cannes

When autumn comes it clears the ocean walk
Of tourists, and the harbor of its yachts.
The merchants meet, the merchants meet and talk
Of anything at all. Heaven dumps its pots.

Now it will rain for weeks. The gleeful gulls
Squeal in the breeze and make continual sport,
While, here below, the season's turbulence lulls
All but the life of cats of every sort,

Who mob the marketplace and do not heed
The fact that human enterprise is ailing.
Is this the price men pay? The merchants plead,

"Save us!" But Mary, trapped in iron paling,
Splashed by the fetid contents of the squall,
High on her sodden hill, moves not at all.

The Helmsmen

We are indifferent to the constant skies
That fostered us and that we once revered,
And sickened by those cities where surprise
Charmed us a little while and disappeared.

We have an old nostalgia for the seas,
And trail the sun westward until its glow
Bleeds on the palms of far Hesperides
While we lie here, windless in Sargasso.

Helmsmen always, our sails are limp and slack.
We take them down and sleep between the folds,
Dreaming at night the splendid voyage back

Into the lands we left. Locked in our holds,
The desperate treasure of unspent desire
Quakes and the crimson seas shall be our pyre.

This Is the World

This is the world, imperfect by design,
Splaying in curls beneath the plowman's feet,
The farmhouse almost strangled by the vine
And almost swallowed by a sea of wheat,

That swells beyond us, rolling all unchecked,
A sanctuary for the rapacious crow,
Where bristling yellow wheat-spears resurrect
The tall mortality of hurt Van Gogh.

That road may twist to Hell, that road may end
In heaps of bones and wheels and broken jars.
Though swirling tides of darkness comprehend

The road, the traveler, the cypress tree,
At last the convoluted moon and stars
Give the benighted world the light to see.

Season of Reprieve

Villon at Meung, 1461

Day's end. A world of mud. The central square
Puddled in sheets. A locked hotel de ville.
Still, in the darkness, someone sloshes there.
Moonbeams, guttering through the clouds, reveal
A sick old man in his thirty-second year.

The bishop locked him up last spring. This hour,
Locked out of jail, the earth becomes his prison.
Worse than jail-damp, forgiveness fouls the air.
The townsfolk hope he won't outlast the season.
He coughs. The raw wind tugs his thin white hair.

Last year he came to town with roving eyes,
Picking their locks and threatening to take
Suzie and Nana for his beggar's prize,
Right in the manner of a Paris rake,
Till the bishop swore to cut him down to size.

But once in jail he wouldn't shrive, and worse,
They saw his will. It was called "a scurrilous thing,
Thoughts from the gutter cast in gutter verse."

They scourged and starved him till the new-crowned king,
Riding through town, revoked the bishop's curse.

He may be wondering which way is best—
Those jagged wheel-ruts down and out of town?
Or back through town, perhaps to beg a crust
Off some poor housewife? No, he's heading down
The ruts, pulling his rags across his chest.

Where will he go now, rheumy, wracked with gout,
His face so pocked and scabbed he looks inhuman?
Children will gawk, and run from him, and shout.
He'll get no bed nor board nor wine nor woman.
He'll cough and cough. Whole towns will drive him out.

Cur with distemper, cudgeled down the road,
Striding like Christ with firm, deliberate steps.
His ragged greatcoat brazens through the cold,
Original rain, into the Great Perhaps,
Caked with the churned-up wallow of the world.

Late Gothic

I.
On a cold night in March
We quarreled, you went to bed, I paced
Down the cobblestone street. All at once I faced
A yellow, wolfish dog
That withered all vanity on sight,
And froze. *Why had we fought?* Slowly, step by step,

I moved backward while he,
Out of the darkness of centuries
Snarling his hate with fangs bared and mouth foaming,
Slowly advanced on me.
Where men founded a faith that moved stone,
One learned what makes hair bristle and the heart stop.

II.
The night wind grips the monastery's eaves,
The ocean cuts her sorrows in the rocks.
Once in that tower above the wind-thrashed seas
A careful brother copied out his books.

Tonight within the mountain something grieves
Under the horologe that beats no tones,
Under the calcified-by-moonlight trees:
A lone dog, hangdog, baying on the stones.

Day at Lucerne

O Lake, O large
Blue vacuum between hills,
No filthy barge

Bisects you. One
Beautiful lady swims
In you, takes sun

On your far shore,
Pagan and barefoot. How
Perfectly sure

She is! The day,
Because of her, tears on,
Nor can she stay:

Your darkening street
Clicks with the rhythm of
Her high-heeled feet.

Two at Zurich

The day being warm we took the cable car
Up to the Dolder's terraced swimming pool.
That afternoon we noticed an old woman
With two white kittens on a leash of ribbon.
She wore a black dress with a frilly bodice
That plunged to show the skin below her neckline
Reddened, obese from years of languishing.
You asked me whether she was Swiss or German.
German, I thought, but surely not a hausfrau.
We had seen her on the excursion boat at Stein.
Of course, you knew I didn't know the answer.
That's why you asked the question — just to see
If I would show annoyance, and I didn't.
The question being a ruse to draw me out,
You didn't have a right to know my mind.
I was fatigued. The water in the pool
Was cool and clear. I plunged in once again
And didn't speak to you for half an hour.
And you resented it, I know. You sat
Cross-legged on the lawn and turned your gaze
To children or the woman dressed in black,
As if to tell me that you didn't care.
The woman too had sat down on the grass,

Gazing with indirection out across
The pool, its edge, and all of its surroundings.
Her look was half-expectant, half-defeated,
As though she had seen some figure in the distance
And now was at a loss to make it out.
And while she sat this way the two white kittens
Played in her black lace petticoats at will,
In lace and out of lace. She didn't stop them
Although they rolled and spat and traded blows.
I climbed out of the water and you asked
If I had seen the kittens in their play.
"What's to become of us?" I asked abruptly.
You sat a moment, motionless, your hands
Clasped round your knees, your eyes upon your toes.
Then in a sudden movement like a shiver
You shook your head just once and that was all.
I fell back in the grass and laid one hand
Across my eyes. I could recall the day
We went to look at Stein, the old stone village,
And you had put a red bow in your hair.
One of the village fools made fun of us.
He trailed and mimicked us till we had gone
Down the long street and darkness had come on
But that red bow still flashed upon your hair . . .
The woman in black had gotten up to go,
Her kittens trailing, catching at her hems.
Who was she but a widow and a stepchild,
Cut loose to wander Europe all alone,
Barren, thick-fleshed, forgotten but still searching,
If only for a drowned man in a pool?
Why had we come up here to do our swimming,
Here on the height, when there's a lake below?
I couldn't think. Zurich was under shadow.

The sunlight dimmed upon the opposite height.
"I'm tired enough to sleep a hundred years,"
I said. And when I wakened, all was darkness.
"Joan, are you there?" I said. There was no answer.
And cursing to myself I trudged toward town.

Liedchen

From Zurich to Milwaukee
The burghers quaff their beer
And crunch their kraut and sausages
And brag about their businesses,
    But O my pretty fräulein,
    What'll we do this year?

I've loved your loving daughter.
We've gone too far, I fear . . .
It has a hollow sound to it?
You haven't come around to it?
    Tell me, what am I doing?
    What am I doing here?

I've had lunch with your father.
He said to reappear
When I had more to show for it.
Till then he wouldn't go for it.
    But O my pretty fräulein,
    What'll we do this year?

After One Hundred Years the True Prince Came

Do you remember the distressful time
When both your parents used to sit and jaw,
Expounding to their would-be son-in-law
Manners and morals, politics and rhyme?

And when the two of them at last were gone,
Taking to bed their chitchat and forced laughter,
Do you remember what occurred thereafter,
O busty fraulein dressed in blue chiffon?

Do you recall those stiff and clubby dances
Where they would watch us, trying to make sure
Our thoughts were upper middle class and pure?
We'd pinch beneath their fond approving glances.

And how, to stay in tune with those affairs,
We braced ourselves with drink, for only drink
Could move our lips to make your parents think
That every virtue in the world was theirs?

And how the two of us would gasp for air,
Out in the night, and far from those successes,

Whose boredom now gave way to those caresses
That made the starry night much lovelier?

And how you turned to me when it was over,
Your eyes imperious and full of light,
And said that though you favored me tonight
Tomorrow you would want another lover?

And how I raged and fumed and hung my head,
And in a priggish temper called you slut?
And how you said that you were nothing but?
And how I hung on all you did and said?

We wander through the night, two separate bodies
In separate orbits. Wander where we will,
No one has matched our light or said what God is.
You feel the other tug you toward him still.

And still the world must crabbedly condemn
Those girls who gave their all and did not marry,
Who let their hasty breathless vows miscarry.
Alas, too soon the years will send to them

Hot flashes in the middle of December,
Spice for their dreams, the ginger of regret,
And on their ample bosoms primly set
Chill stones in mid-July. Will they remember

The amorous, wakeful boys that love them yet?
How in the name of love could they forget?

The Ballad of Dead Yankees

Where's Babe Ruth, Sultan of Swat,
Who rocked the heavens with his blows?
Grabowski, Pennock, and Malone—
Mother of mercy, where are those?

Where's Tony (Poosh 'em up) Lazzeri,
The quickest man that ever played?
Where's the gang that raised the roof
In the house that Colonel Ruppert made?

Where's Lou Gehrig, strong and shy,
Who never missed a single game?
Where's Tiny Bonham, where's Jake Powell
And many another peerless name?

Where's Steve Sundra, good but late,
Who for a season had his fling?
Where are the traded, faded ones?
Lord, can they tell us anything?

Where's the withered nameless dwarf
Who sold us pencils at the gate?

Hurled past the clamor of our cheers?
Gone to rest with the good and great?

Where's the swagger, where's the strut,
Where's the style that made the hitter?
Where's the pitcher's swanlike motion?
What in God's name turned life bitter?

For strong-armed Steve, who lost control
And weighed no more than eighty pounds,
No sooner benched than in his grave,
Where's the cleverness that confounds?

For Lou the man, erect and clean,
Wracked with a cruel paralysis,
Gone in his thirty-seventh year,
Where's the virtue that was his?

For nimble Tony, cramped in death,
God knows why and God knows how,
Shut in a dark and silent house,
Where's the squirrel quickness now?

For big brash Babe in an outsize suit,
Himself grown thin and hoarse with cancer,
Still autographing balls for boys,
Mother of mercy, what's the answer?

Is there a heaven with rainbow flags,
Silver trophies hung on walls,
A horseshoe grandstand, mobs of fans,
Webbed gloves and official balls?

Is there a power in judgment there
To stand behind the body's laws,
A stern-faced czar whose slightest word
Is righteous as Judge Kenesaw's?

And if there be no turnstile gate
At that green park, can we get in?
Is the game suspended or postponed?
And do the players play to win?

Mother of mercy, if you're there,
Pray to the high celestial czar
For all of these, the early dead,
Who've gone where no ovations are.

Son of Stone

July, the little ears of corn
Were dying on the stalk. I drove
Across the land where I was born,
Out of luck and out of love.

One of my friends had been divorced,
Was sick at giving up his daughter;
And one in jail appeased his thirst
Not with Beaujolais but water.

Another friend no help could stead;
At twenty-five his bullet went
Singing through his massive head;
He lost the lyric argument.

A woman that I hoped to marry
Had left me to my gloomy mind
The previous year in January.
Yes, and I had an older friend

Whose trust in me I had betrayed
Although I thought myself exempt

From such a deed. For this I paid
With an excess of self-contempt,

And lived without a hope or plan,
On monthly credit from the folks,
Till like a ruined businessman
Who drops his face, forgets his jokes,

I boarded up my whole concern
In any way I could and drove
Across the land where I was born
Out of luck and out of love.

Bad Days

Those days were like the country's politics,
Steamy and rank and full of dirty tricks.
So hot, you heard the corn grow all night long,
The natives said, and they were not far wrong.
Girls sauntered by with almost nothing on.
All things were joggled in the midday sun.
One lugged beer cases, struggling to compete
With men who slid like zombies through the heat . . .

Jesus, I guess we're in it now for life.
The cat, the baby, and the pregnant wife
Are paying for the world's mismanagement.
Sun pounds the roof but they are innocent.
What can one say to those who like their dreams,
The world is not the hellhole that it seems?
Fat chance. Tonight I'll sit in Kenney's, drink
Weak beer, sweat rhymes, and give it one more think . . .

While, on the tube, that puffed-up senator
Postures and grunts "Ahem" to get the floor,
"A point of order, point of order here!"
Then fouls both men and rules, a piggish leer
Stuck on his face to show him full of wit,
Drunk and enamored of his brand of shit.
Oh, say, *sow-ee, sow-ee* of thee we sing,
Our patriotic pig, our cornball king!

Current Events

A faucet in the kitchen sink is dripping.
Slowly the minutes pass, the day drags out.
At six o'clock men quiz their wives about
The remote possibility of stripping.

No need to back it up with last week's clipping,
This is the latest trend without a doubt.
Oh, life is leaking through a water spout,
And many a man has told himself, "I'm slipping."

Though politics of course is here to stay—
Housing, finance, corruption, and decay,
The fate of China and the Second Coming—

My dear, unless the husbands have their way,
The steady dripping that we hear today
Will grow tomorrow to a steady drumming.

Country Tavern

I.
It stood beside a river,
Under some willow trees.
A nineteen-thirty flivver
Had sunk by slow degrees

Into the river bed
That now was caked and dried.
Neon blue and red
Lit up the place inside.

Upon a sawdust floor
Two women I had seen
In a nightmare once before
Danced, as an old machine

Wheezed out a polka. In
One corner of the room
Strangely familiar men
Were huddled, each of whom

Sucked at a glass of beer
As though it were his last.

Two mounted heads of deer
Recalled from seasons past

Those days of fortitude
When hunter, dog, and hunted
Pursued and were pursued
And knew what life they wanted.

II.
One was a feather-white and one was spotted.
One had a rhythmic step, the other not.

One was a mother twice but gave it up
When nothing ever seemed to come out right.
She was a hen and labored all day long
To keep a house and tend a little plot.
Her children buried and her garden blighted,
She lost herself in dancing day and night.

One was a pampered child and one was hated.
One had a clucking voice, the other brayed.

One had a kind of knot within her breast
That from her childhood only grew more tight.
She was a mule and had no use for men.
And shunned by women, till she found the hen
She had not found in life a thing she wanted.
And now she lived by dancing day and night.

III.
There was a dancing mule
Who traveled with a hen

Each, a burning whole,
Had had enough of men.

So they stuck together
And held each other tight
Through fair or stormy weather,
Morning, noon, and night.

While they did their dance
A group of men sat by,
Playing at games of chance,
Pale, humorless, dry,

Who uttered growls and cursed
God or the Black Prince
For having made such thirst
Out of their impotence.

One played euchre and dice,
Being bored with life,
And lost his portion twice,
Losing land and wife.

Another one, who chased
After womankind,
Found them sly, two-faced,
Charming a man blind

But taking none for mate.
Perched on a high stool,
He spat out his hate
At the hen and the dancing mule.

And still another one,
Whose heart was free of crime,
Lost his wits in the sun
Once in a far-off time;

The sweet heat laid him low,
Face down in his domain,
Where grasshopper and crow
Lunched in the noonday grain.

All who were defeated —
The dancing mule and the hen,
Their passion unabated,
The desperate countrymen

Whom nature had dismissed,
Those who gambled and drank,
Those with a sensual twist —
Rank upon sullen rank

Were gathered in this hall
In mutual disgrace,
Where one who looked at all
Found his own face.

IV.
Dangerous summer, powdering the grain
With dried-up topsoil, blowing in the grain
With a dry crackle, I can still recall
Farmers who prayed and waited for the rain
And then found nothing but an early fall:

A crop of thistles blooming in the heart
Of things, till each one bore it in his heart.
Pitiless beauty, how should I dispraise
Those whom you tried to stifle from the start?
Caught for a short while in your hot blue gaze,

They knew such dissolution of their pride
They spoke of nothing but the dust of pride,
Too weak to stop their ruin and too late.
For them a team of horses lived and died.
A dry wind moved them like an unlatched gate.

Winter Journey

At unmarked crossroads, all that afternoon,
We could see the fences sifting snowdrifts,
And the frame houses that looked like mere

Extensions of landscape, whited, solitary,
Yet always ringed by a few spare trees
And furrow on dry furrow stopped with snow.

And while we watched, occasionally the wind
Rose from the land, vesting itself in snow,
And fell back once more in flurried silence.

Only a hurt god, tangled in the branches
And caught in the crisp weeds, stared out
From that emaciated land, begging our mercy,

Forever beseeching our numbed attentions
With gestures none of us could decipher . . .
His features shifting, untouchable, unreal.

So we peered into that afternoon, late, until
The windows frosted over with our breathing,
And sleep came on, and our high foreheads bowed.

Triptych

I.

I was apprenticed young,
    A shut-in with no sense
Of sunlight or clear sky
    Or the world's experience.

I practiced the devices
    The clever scholars use
To fabricate a garment
    For the sacred Muse.

So all day long I wove
    A pretty metaphor,
Till one night in a dream,
    Through a half-open door,

I fancied that I saw
    A stately woman come
Whose daring and whose grace
    Dazzled my little room.

Oh, life is not the same,
    I must at last confess,

Since first I followed her
    In fear and nakedness.

II.
I must now say goodbye,
As my Muse thinks best,
To the worst pigsty
In the whole Midwest,

Where youth's lofty vision
Blows off its top,
And God's right reason
Goes for hog slop.

To the academic sow
That my old friends follow,
Goodbye now,
Sunk in the wallow.

Goodbye to my youth,
To childhood's star,
To the full-dressed truth.
I have come this far

By courtesy and luck
And long apprenticeship.
Why should I suck
At an old sow's tit?

III.
Of your great store
Grant me this one

Request before
My song is done;

I ask it for
My father's son,
Saint Metaphor,
O sacred Pun:

That by your kind
And winning grace
He shall be heard,

That he may find
In the right place
The right word.

Songs on a Theme

I.

Slid summer underneath her cold inversion,
With sunny slopes and crowded canopies,
      But we were happy.

Come winter without tears that when they freeze
Can pierce the summer-keeping heart and be
      Forever dripping.

Desire these days, my dear, that we may be
Two ever shifting dunes of fine white snow,
      Made one completely.

II.

O come with me, my dear,
Across the ragged meadows,
Into a grove where Care
Sprawls beneath the elms.
Head in the rampant grass,
Bewildered by the shadows
Of wagging leaves, he dreams
And in his dream forgets
What boundaries we trespass.

No sighs of forced regret,
No angry suspirations,
Will aggravate that spot.
In winter, stunning snows
Over us shall undulate,
And subject to the passions
That summertime bestows,
We shall be profligate,
Like shy and perfect fauns.

A breeze that hardly blows
Is whispering *Vivāmus*
There, in those distant boughs
That fan the sunlit air:
Vivāmus O Vivāmus
Where all is light and promise,
Calm breath and soft repose.
O come with me, my dear,
Across the ragged meadows.

III.
When April comes and lets those limbs
Be with bird and apple blossom heavy,
I shall come calling: I cry you praise
     That you who bore winter
     Should bear such beauty.

And when the season lets the grass
Be with quill and fallen petal heavy,
I shall come calling: I cry you praise
     That you who bore beauty
     Should bear such fruit.

And when October swells the breeze
With apple brandy, and the tang is heavy,
I shall come calling: Sweet death, I cry
        You praise. I long to fly
        Into your high branches.

Outrageous Autumn

When the flesh of summer piecemeal mars the lawn
And the tall white house perks smokily among
The skeletal branches, when comer Jack has stung
A few late crabs and the hummingbird is gone,

When milkweed shakes her heavy pod at the sun
That works a paling grin, when the backward worm
Is backward slid and the mole is stuck for a term
In his hole—when dun earth and raw sky are one—

What mind of mine will comprehend the wind
That elbows through the ribs of naked trellises,
That irks the testy leaves and leaves them pinned

In thickets—wind that trumpets rimes and fallacies
And hails the draggled acorns to the ground,
That croons in chimneys with a doomsday sound,

That sneezes up the skirts of tombs and palaces?

Hysteria

The landlocked lake desires the meadow.
The lone dog snaps at his own shadow.

The clockwork stars are wound and set
The moonstruck moth is in a net.

The bridegroom raves. The bags are packed.
Cold Daphne shuns the burning act.

Night falls. Fond Echo pines and pales.
Oblivion fogs the hills and vales.

Over the peaked roofs, leaf by leaf,
A thin, high moan of endless grief.

And, at the springs we settled by,
Narcissus, blooming mad, must die.

The Turning Hill

Go to the wooded hilltop
The chorus of hedges is brown.
The ragweed tells her fullness
To the broken summer sun.

Sorrow will receive you,
Couched in the dry grass
Greeting you in the lost cry
Of many a woodland voice.

Go to the wooded hilltop,
Ripening for the fall.
Sorrow will receive you.
Atop the turning hill

See the village dark and quiet,
Her children — the old story —
Gone like the red and yellow leaves.
Oh, what was their hurry?

Kids at Play

Jump-Rope Rhymes

I.
Time for supper, cold and dark.
There was playing in the park.

There was laughter though the day
Had come to nothing. It was gay.

It was crazy, it was dark.
It was playing in the park.

World so secret, night so deep,
It was time to eat and sleep.

Naughty children. It was fun.
Go home, go home, there's no more sun.

II.
On the playground, in the street,
Careless children gather heat.

In their heads a crazy voice:
Eat fire, eat fire, or turn to ice.

Booms in the sky a big bass drum:
Eat fire, eat fire till Kingdom Come.

Chicken Little, break and fly.
I touched a piece of falling sky.

Hi diddle-diddle. Come what may,
Turn to ash and blow away.

Lines Suggested by Two Monets

I.
It is perhaps a Sunday afternoon.
Four sailboats lie near shore with listless sails,
Caught in a *fin de siècle* sort of calm.
One sees two country homes (where nothing's stirring),
A little dock, some trees, a strip of lawn.

The summer sky has turned ethereal blue,
A huge monotonous nothing. Half the scene
Is purely dull. But look—the rest is water,
Supple, alive, uncaged, where the dead sails
In big reflected splashes dance and writhe.

Season of lassitude, so falsely calm—
Who cares what happens to your Sunday sailors
(Notice how casually they are defined)
When hauling down their sails they straggle home
Never to know their place in history?

II.
Things shuddered into flux. New lies. New men.
Huge guns. "The life of the imagination"?—
Unreal, impractical, too far from life.

Monet, in his backyard, dammed up a stream
By which he lay to hold his meditations.

A time for engineering or maybe
A time for statesmanship. At last a time
To fight the war to end wars. Ranks of boys
Spilled in the thrust and counterthrust.
No time, at any rate, for idle reverie.

Broad-hatted, bearded, head by forearm braced . . .
With water lilies, irises, and blades
In the still interplay of light and shadow,
Back and forth, easy and slow, he made
A tremulous peace that was, is, and will be.

III.
Father, you fought that war, came home and sketched
An old unwarlike France . . . mill-ponds and -wheels,
Great oaks and little farms . . . strong pastoral scenes
That Mother came on when she cleared the attic;
Untouched by time or man's artillery.

I know so little about you and me.
But for the blind luck of the genes' encounter,
Nothing at all would be, not even the years
When only fickle breezes upon water
Rippled the surface that we looked into.

Years come and go. The poet, clowning or angry,
Has no serenity though the world craves it
More than all poems have the power to say.
You said: find your own life. Your sketches hang
In my son's bedroom, near the two Monets.

Mr. Hartley's Diamond Jubilee

He sits alone looking out.

I.

My friends, my sister, my brother, we have been naughty.
The time for supper is past, the village clock
Has rung the hour, our meal is cold on the platter,
And yet we dally, here on the frozen lake.
Up in the village, lost in the lull of the hour,
The lights are long since gone from each little shop,
And the proprietor, busy not now as before,
Is home in an armchair smoking his evening pipe.

And yet we sweep and glide and dally and twitter.
Perhaps we shall be punished for staying at play
This late and this dark, marking time with the weather,
Marking a drowned boy's window with our skates.
Are you still there? Perhaps there will be no supper.
The bell has called us back from the frozen lake.

II.

At play in the drifting snow, in winter wraps,
The secret of burning is all wound in wool,
A knocking, rushing potion. See how it escapes

And fades like vapors rising from the boil.
As winter whines in corners, creaks and claps
My loosened shutter, whistles past my sill,
Breath flies invisibly through my blue lips.
On bitter days the pine trees hardly smell.

Then raise the glasses to the green green holly.
Fair friends grow cold, much love is suffering.
Run out, my dears, run out, my dears, and sing.
Come, winter, puff your belly, freeze and blow.
Look at the burning elfkins! Aren't we jolly.
We play our clockwise games in the drifting snow.

III.
I see a snowman on the neighbor's lawn
(With a ha, ha, hey!) with charcoal eyes.
A wintry blast will laugh about his chin,
And birds, dull birds, make impish pleasantries.
He ought to lose his temper but he won't.
Perhaps he's grown so elderly and wise
That the weather has become his element.
A wintry blast will set him at his ease.

The sky is surly. Dull birds chirp, not sing.
All winters snowball into one. The squirrel
Is boon companion where I stick and ponder.
What sets the pine boughs in a blustery quarrel
And stops the gush of any dripping thing
Has mouthed its impudence on the winter window.

Going Back

I.
Just where my long road started out, it ends.
I stand alone and see my childhood town
Calling its kids and saying goodnight to friends.
And now the tasseled window shades draw down.

Old men and women, slumped in easy chairs,
Fold up their papers, yawn, and cease to talk.
I know that only a tireless streetlamp cares
Where I, a ghost with fisted pockets, walk.

Shadow and I, we play a little game
Of hide-and-seek, as we have always done.
Some years ago I had a boy's nickname,
Voiced in this street and known by everyone.

That name, those years, companions that I had—
Channing the fiddler and the girls next door,
The roughneck gang that drove my father mad,
Trampling his flowers in their relentless war—

Where are they now, so dear and out of date?
Old men and women yawn but do not stir

The burned-out embers, and the hour is late.
Someone is calling but I can't see her.

"Sneakthief!" she cries. "You've waited here too long,
  Thinking of them, beneath an old streetlamp.
  Shadow will fall on you, and he will throng
  Your reckless head and beat you for a tramp.

"And when you go back home — to your own home —
  No one will know you. Peering through a crack,
  Familiar eyes will say, 'At last you've come.'
  Familiar eyes will say, 'You can't come back.'"

II.
Home is a place of resurrections. Fears
I ran away from, sorrows that I fled,
Come back to haunt me now from other years.
Two neighbors I remember best are dead.

There was a mean and bitter-hearted man
Who murdered songbirds in his orchard plot
And dropped their bodies in a garbage can.
In memory of the songbirds that he shot

My fancy likes to languish and delay
Beside the lilacs where the gang would meet.
Knickered, distracted from our usual play,
We planned our vengeance. Down the quiet street,

Elm-shadowed, cool, my fancy likes to browse
Where Mr. Slemmons sang his tenor part
On Sundays in his good green-gabled house
With wife and kids, till stricken in the heart,

He lost life's tune before the tune went sour.
Now dead some years, his operatic voice
Seems mingled with the songbirds'. Hour on hour
I hear them singing as the spectral boys

Steal from the orchard with unblemished pears,
Ambrosial apples, sacrificial plums.
They speak in breathless tones, yet no one cares.
No keeper of the orchard ever comes

To kill the songbirds. On the highest limb
A ghostly blue jay wrangles with a leaf,
But no one hears the cry that bursts from him
Except myself. He cries, "Sneakthief, sneakthief!"

The Stages of Narcissus

I.

Was it his face that so unsettled him,
Fluid and changeable and childly wise?
One day he watched a water spider skim
Across the pool. His image met his eyes,
And changing as the water's surface changed,
It filled him with a shiver of delight.
He thought that all his life had been arranged
By some unwished-for providence. He might
Go on pretending that he didn't know,
But people in their drawing rooms would show
Him as a thing of some refinement, sought
For taste or wit or common sense alone,
While in their secret cells they railed and fought
Like wild dogs tearing at a bloody bone.

II.

Take any subway to the nearest place:
He is standing like a statue in the crowd.
And schoolgirls titter when they see his face
Dejected, overserious, soft, and proud.
They edge about him in the evening press,
Sudden as sparks struck from electric rails.

In him they sense a kind of tenderness
At which the heart despairs. The current fails,
The lights go out. Feeling strange in his clothes,
Down through the neural passageways he goes,
Groping his way till all at once a door
Snaps open, and a snarling fair-haired beast
Bursts through the breach. The lights come on once more,
Offering the body to the sensual feast.

III.
Daylong upon the baked or windy street
The passing citizens would seem like flies
Engulfing him, till at his restless feet
The very pavement bristled with their eyes.
If night was kind to him it made his face,
Beneath its glow, an amber-lighted bronze,
And gave his form a more than human grace.
At evening in the park, beside the ponds,
He walked among the statues who were dumb,
Who could not hear his step or tell him from
Those solid citizens, the sculptured dead.
But from the benches of the fenced-in park
The eyes bugged out at him and made him dread
The will to live that paralyzed the dark.

IV.
Had he foreseen, since that discovery day,
The nature and the passion of his fall?
The sunlight beats the panes but will not stay.
He shuts his eyes and feels the bedroom wall
Fill up with shadow till his life seems trapped
As in some narrow subterranean flaw,
In which he lies awake, raw nerves unsnapped,

Alive and throbbing. Did he know the law
That ties a man in knots but leaves him whole,
Coupling the flesh in marriage with a soul
That shrieks, "Whoever touches me I hate—
I shall assume the rectitude of stone,"
Then drinks the fiery blood and knows her mate,
Submissive to the flesh she claimed to own?

V.
Echo half slept. She watched her wished-for one
Drift through the woods with his impassive mask.
But was it he or their potential son,
The hoped fulfillment of her earthly task?
She didn't know. All night he never spoke
And she would watch him. Then, as sunrise sprung
Out of the east, he sank away. She woke,
Moaning the verses of an ancient song—
She who could have no life save through another:
"O that you were familiar as my brother
   That sucked my mother's breasts. Then I would kiss you.
   I'd flutter round you like a little swallow
   And lead you to my mother's house. She'd bless you.
   I'd pour you wine. And where you went I'd follow."

VI.
Shall earth, the bone collector, drag to rot
The flowers that she labored to upraise?
In blushful belles the rarest beauty spot
Glows but a day, blood ranging in the face,
At last relinquished to an old gravure,
While, on the couch of earth, the grave worm plows
The flesh, that was the soul's investiture,
Kissing the lips, the Grecian nose, the brows,

Cruising along the contours of each limb . . .
That night he dreamed a woman followed him,
Calling him softly by his childhood name.
He turned, and in an ecstasy of flight,
Went scampering down the street till she became
Less than a whisper dying through the night.

VII.

My true reflection, likeness not quite real,
My image, all reversed, my silent half—
You sneer and think yourself a man of steel,
And when I laugh at you, you ape my laugh.
I turn my back on you, you turn your back.
You seem to keep in perfect time with me.
You are possessor of the things I lack.
I burn, and you are cool and maidenly.
If I were you I would be steel, my fears
Nothing but shadows in a house of mirrors.
But I am not. Each backward step you take
Tells me, your maker, of your arrogance.
You love me and you love me not. You make
A mockery of me as you dance my dance.

VIII.

Why should paternal heaven wish to keep
This shadow that a mirror cannot hold?
Better to lose oneself in a stone sleep
Than bear the indignity of growing old.
And what if sculptors cut you from the stone
And stand you up before the general eye?
O then a real indifference comes on,
Locked in the stone, descended from the sky,
Ascended from the windings of the earth . . .

By the still pool he had his second birth,
Studying his imagery in fateful springs.
He leaned and looked, hunching his long spine.
Kissing his face, he shivered it in rings.
And the dream passed in broken water shine.

IX.
Where does the form go when it disappears?
Into a pool whose depth no man may tell;
Into a wellspring's throat, the pit of years;
Into the always churning floods of hell.
It goes to join the spun world at the source,
All form being changed to movement there below,
Tumbling from cave to cave until its force
Speaks in the taproots of the flowers that blow.
Maiden, beside what fountain do you dare
To pick this flower and flaunt it in your hair?
Here lies the virgin boy, bound in his bed
With no fair love, no marriageable heart;
By day the world pursued him and he fled
To its dark night where the clear waters start.

Early and Late

We struggled in the lines and stood with them all,
Thirty-five years and more. Here let us pause.

Some of our numbers faltered, some of them fell
Out, though we fought for them all about equally.

Some of them struck their blows in service of truth,
Doing their duty, some were diseased with affection.

One lady fell, one lively childlike mischief.
One student tried to lift her, one weak student,

Who ever afterward, recalling how
She grinned at him, was prone to tears and laughter.

Live, she demanded his attention. Dead,
She overwhelmed the boy. He burned. He froze.

The winter winds were nothing to the winds
That stung within him, thinking of the lady.

He shook with tears and laughter in his loins
Till sick to death he joined her in repose.

Two roses then—one white, one crimson—grew
Out of their graves. Enough of it? Let go.

For who can speak the woe of man and woman?
The fluent one becomes a stammerer.

Some readers might inquire, "What fuss is this?
Things never seemed so heavy, not in this world."

Give them an older book that will remind them
Not of Bruce and the spider that tried and tried,

But the finished web, looking deceptively easy—
Not of those who died for the freedom to speak

As their ancestors had, but the new meanings wound
In the accustomed devices, the roses intertwined.

Smiling for Foggerson

Graduation Photo

Sunlight shafts through the late primaveral air
As you stand, looking back, on the stair.
It lights in your hair on the perfect hair part
Where your skin has the whiteness of fish. It drowns
In the bronze of your face, in the pitch of your eyes,
Where glints and flashes of it dart below.
A triangle of it shines on your fortified bust.
A curve of it graces your buttocks supple and full.
A facet of it lies on your ankle bone
Whose delicate movements are mankind's undoing.

You smile as if you could guess what Foggerson knows
And will not, for fear of spoiling the pose, declare:
That the pleats in your skirt will never need ironing,
That your bracelet bangles will jingle no more,
That the cashmere sweater over the good foundation
Will never come off again for any reason
Or show any signs of wear, that your natural teeth
In their natural box will never chatter or tarnish.
In the midst of life we *are* in death:
The death's head shows through the Cupid's bows.

So smile till we know how much of your skull is teeth.
Foggerson sees you always, just as you are,
Though you lose all recollection of him
And droop, sag, whiten, and settle in dust.
He is not even part of your shadow, but only in him
Will you be perfect, this moment, here. Now go
And still smile. Smile till the lines in your face
Deepen and set in a conventional scowl.
Scowl down the years till the years
Are frozen and you can no longer dissemble:
Before this you were nothing, and nothing after.

But along with it all, and more than it all, this You—
The hope, the longing, the fulfillment—
Smiling not because anyone prodded you to,
But lips parted in joy of expectation,
As if just at this moment came to you
The invisible shuttle that slithers through the years,
Threading the furthest stars,
Aimed at you, for once, now whirling in you.
Quick now, it's going to be
A good one—there, you've done it together.
On Foggerson's black plate you will live forever.

Great Bay

Is the moon's impetuous friend whom the moon eggs on
Like a liberation leader demanding,
"Come on, show me your action."

Is a great protein factory. Clams, crabs, mussels,
Flat fish or round swell the roundness
She shows the barren moon.

Is a still where the dead age slowly, is a speaker
Pumping hymns till Dad says, "Drink,"
And all the small fry drown.

The waves drone in, ignoring business, traffic,
Barber shops, baseball games, and prayers.
"Hallelujah," sing the clams

In chaplets of bubbles winding from the bottom.
In Great Bay one can hear no crack
Of a gun, no thud, no suck

Of the flesh through a rupturing metal tube into
Dark space, only a skittery *skreak*
Inside, and outside, only

A slopping and sloshing of things forever awash,
A grand impatience that takes no guff
But dwells on crudities,

Including, scudding her black waves, the gulls
Screeching, kids scouting her white shoals,
Red-eyed and spluttering,

And boys and girls riding the hissing foam
On boards, who sleep on the far beach,
Driving the blood home—

Insouciant of that fabulous, iron-banded
Treasure, still lying uninvested,
That in these precincts hides,

A cache of blood, guts, greed, clutched wholly to
Itself, earning no interest but
From worms or barnacles,

Until, the lease on its long oblivion lapsing,
Earth hawks it up. The tale is endless
Savagery. Great Bay

Is the fecund tub and maelstrom out of which
All spins, the vortex of the End
That winches all back in,

As Mrs. Jenks cranks in the morning wash line
Of pants, skirts, shorts, and other bits
That cover breasts and loins.

Is camp and playground and secret breeding place
Where Heaven and Earth begot the gods,
Where the first worm-like men

Squirmed from the ashes, where the next, sky-shouting,
Naked, shameless men made way
For one unregenerate poet

Brazening through the rain, for monarchs, their consorts,
Their eunuchs and painters and doomsayers,
Pirates, fools, torturers,

Those that scourge the flesh, that turn the screws,
That slice the flesh with maniacal laughter,
Leaving a man without beads,

A homeless hermit dithering along the beaches.
"Hallelujah, hallelujah," sing the clams
In twisting bubbles. Cash

Trays of shining pebbles spill in on the spume,
Click-click, while dead men reconnoiter
The depths and make rendezvous,

But strangely reticent, make no new transactions,
In no rush, over a bottle of black
Dead men's rum. "Hallelujah,"

Sing the boys and girls, their registers ringing,
Their blood brewed by the kissing foam.
"Hallelujah, we are home."

Women of the Hour

I.
Pamela rose at five A.M. She leaned into
Her mirror and thought, "At least *I* live, if nothing does.

"What's more, I know I lived last night, in party clothes.
I teased my curls and looked and wondered, *Whose long face*

Is that I see, whose pose? If those conjectures all
Are now dry bones, who am I now?" She pattered out

Upon her folks' verandah, viewed the scented dew-cup
Posies, and touched this one, this pink *I am*, this Pam.

Here, for a wink, she lives, in dawn's pink-shadowed quiet.
She lives and breathes and is, and no one may deny it.

II.
Suzanne sat up at ten
    In Dr. Van Atta's office
"Yes, Suzanne, you're all right
    Now, though it may be a while
Before you can do *every*-
    thing you used to do . . .

Though your most immediate problem's
    Gone, a deeper one
Lies underneath your skin,
    Your well-proportioned surface."

"Oh, doctor, thanks. But save it,
    Though. I gave and I got.
I got what I couldn't keep,
    And yes, it's paid and done.
Tell me — you know my problem —
    I feel nifty, no?
What ails you, Dr. Van?
    Haven't you ever loved
A woman, child, or man,
    Stuck in your bloody office?"

III.

Sarah unhooked at ten P.M.
    The straps of another woman.
"Come and be free, confide in me.
    Tell me your story, I'll tell my own.
Don't lie all alone and hold it all in,
    But try to see the you in me.
We're one in faith and bound to no man,
    This is our body and our blood.
Now, what would you like me to do," said she,
    "For all that is kind and human?"

IV.

Carolyn came at ten-fifteen,
    Breathless and flushed. The wall was breached,
The sea broke through: the raging, earth-
    impounded sea, through break after break,

Burst on the fields with salt and wet,
    Letting out torment, letting out hate,
And soon, lying flat and perfectly still,
    Still moon-kept and all stretched out
The whole world's length, laid on the land
    An audacious hand, and slept.

V.
Sister Francine at six-fifteen
    Woke with a prayer:
"Praise to my father the butcher, who taught
    My brother to cleave
The blocks of meat—praise to my brother,
    Smeared with the gore,
Performing the deed. Praise to our mother
    Who willingly bore
My other brother the druggist and my
    Two married sisters.
From duties to sleeping to waking, praise
    The thought that runs
Through us and connects us, wherever
    We are, and always,
All in one. Then praise to chance
    And to anti-chance,
To plants and to insects, the inmost weave of
    Their being, the dance
Of their seasonal coming and going—what drove
    Them to consciousness
Drives me too, though in me it strangely
    Accrues in these words,
In my choice, in this now, as I can speak it:
    Hush, dear, *tais-toi*:
In mind of this being that shines on the ground

Of your understanding,
In praise of this living and dying, in thanks
For this blood, be still."

Walking Along the Hudson

Catskill, New York

The fat friar stroking golf balls
Has lost one of them in a bush.
We ask, may we look at the grounds?
"Oh, they come through here with cahs," says he,
And goes after the golf ball.

On the bluff's height stands the Friary,
Immaculate in yellow brick
And circled with a ribbon of asphalt, freshly laid.
If God is not here He is not anywhere.
(Yes, and the Holy Ghost is freshly laid.)

Beyond the tended lawn and the tennis courts,
Where does the spirit turn for exercise?
To the very edge of the bluff—
Down ruined steps and past a crumbling fountain
Where the old order stood, through trees
Older than any evidence of man,
The path of meditation winds through shade
To the knoll of prayer standing in full view
Of a field of water cabbage

And the many-prismed Hudson with its danger rock,
Its barges and their drones,
Reborn, made right, washed clean
In the blows of the sun—
To the pool of stinks, effluvium of friars,
God's sluice, the putrid spring,
Where those who pass by
Feel drawn into hell by their gut-strings,
Where the spirits of flatulence live out their lives
Wandering filmily through ferns and sumacs,
Inspiring stinkbugs and blowflies,
Where the traveler, reeling in fumes, stupid and lost,
Nevertheless clings to the narrowing path
And observes, from the undermined cliff,
A graveyard of trees,
Huge trunks broken off like chalk,
Lying, elephant-colored, on the rocks;
And then the steep path upward,
Head swimming with heat,
And the thorns and creepers and branches
That snatch at your flesh as if to say,
"Don't go away! Don't go away!
You who pass by us to eternity,
Show us your pity!
If, as the breezes cry,
We have no being save in your consciousness,
Gaze on us, that we may exist—for see
(Ah, see), how we die."

At Lake Desolation

Saratoga County, New York. Good Friday, 1971

Ten miles out
And how far in?
Shore rimmed by scrub pine, scrub birch,
And first-growth hemlock, passed over
As of no worth
By lumber crews.
Roadsides heaped with snow, the kettle-round lake
Ice-bound, a few
Winterized cottages, snug in their little smokes. Not
Like the Mohawks who
Captured Isaac and "caressed" him with coals . . .
"Unhappy infidels
Whose lives are passed in smoke, and their eternity
In flames of Hell."
Dour Saint Isaac—in your black book, in your long black
Soutane sweeping
Across the snow, they saw only Death, ruined crops, famine,
The black plague.
To exorcise you, to shake off your power, to make you
No more than man,

They dragged you to Ossernenon,
They burned and slashed you. Abashed by your
Silence, called
In their squaws,
Who tore out your nails with their teeth, with a clam
Shell worked off
Your thumb. Your mouth, before they hacked off your head,
Did it cry out
That this was not for the first time? Three
Hundred years,
And, *contra naturam*, here's
The evergreen
First-growth
Hemlock, a lean spray of it
Picked by us
Bloodlessly,
Not for the first or last time but forever.
Such is the trespass and the violation.

Upstate Lilacs

Up the spring hillside where the dug road went
Before the county realigned it, past
Broken stone walls and grown-up fields, we find
The old foundations folding. Round about them
The lilacs stand, stiffly, with none to please
Or take account of. By the ruined sills
They wave their heart-shaped leaves and shake
    their blooms,
Flouting the fact that those who planted them
Gave up the homestead. If the shallow wells
Went foul, if rains and snows of yesteryear
Escaped the catchments, if the summer sun
Turned on the crops, leaving the fields burnt straw,
If three hard winters cracked the will to plough,
Or if, simply, there was no special reason
To stay on high ground when the Indians
That held the river valley had moved on,
We cannot know, although these old maids might,
These gnarled old maids, the hardiest of whom
Stand round about in green and lavender,
Heedless of man, preferring their perfume.

Croquet Me Far Beyond

Croquet me far beyond the furthest wicket—
No matter where I lie, O my blue-striped,
Imperious lady, I will lie for you.

As for the others, I am sick of them—
Out of position, dead on them, and stuck,
Time and again knocked and used by them.

Knocked, used, blasted out, bypassed,
I've made my wicket! Now to get the others.
I'm back in business and they're going to pay.

Take that, Yellow. Take that, Red. And you,
You simpering Purple, you're the one who first
Spoiled my position at the middle wicket—

Take that!

To be or not to be, this moment, King?
To lose a crown but gain the world, maybe?
How best to seize upon these chances and choices?

Poison, I have knocked the others off,
And now the field is down to me and you.
If you're going to knock me off, be quick about it . . .

Something about the day, the way it closes
On stakes and wickets, something about the dusk
On new mown grass, here in the Kindest Kingdom . . .

Diurnal hubbub done, celestial bodies
Whirling in concert on eternal turf,
Of whom, as moon to earth, we two make one.

Solitary Woman

Close was enough, but any closer,
   More than you could bear.
      Seated inside,

Eating, I, a sometime talker often
   Struck dumb, glimpsed you
      And shuddered,

Considering the glory of your estate:
   To wait always hungrily
      At the Great Door.

If one had kept you under a gentle
   Thumb when you were younger,
      If one had not

Let you taste the bruised black
   Radishes dabbled in shoyu
      And attar of sesame,

If one had not at first unfolded, then
   Pulled out from under you
      The Khalabar,

It would have been different. As it was,
     Glancing inside, you paused,
          Sensing the threshold.

So it was not without forbearance,
     Refusing to be admitted,
          You had come.

The Moon Man

Minding this fallen world, kicking its leaves,
Waiting for something to happen, fearing what might,
Infected with life yet having no wish to transmit it,
One walks along in the autumn, kicking dead leaves.

Torn from us, mourned for, consigned to the earth,
The long friends lie in a hard box out of sight.
Tomorrow, beached on the dark side of the moon
In a sealed can: complete mummification.
Or let the burial missile nudge past the moon,
That the dead may continue to wander.

> *O deep dark outer space — in you*
> *All objects shine more beautifully than on earth.*
> *We have sought you in pools and looking glasses,*
> *We have called conventions in your name,*
> *We have found you in powders and in drink.*
> *Mad with your ether we have hit the moon.*

How many years, mooning around inside me, a man
Droller than myself claims he can't act without
Further instructions. Sly, cantankerous loon —
I'm done humoring you. Out the door with you, out.

Out, at the town's end. Out. Save what you can.
Scratch in the dust with the long tines plinking,
Tinka-tink-ting, by the bonfire's towering fumes.
And rake what is foul to a pure acrid burning.

Certain Vers Librists

They're so broad-minded they might *like* what I'm
About to say: "In plain American,
The language of the streets, let's praise the time
When Harry, plucky rooster, gave 'em hell."

But no, my foot gets in their way. It balks them.
Like this, it goes. And this. See how the line
Comes halting forth. One might trip over it.
And limp off, sore, nursing the bad, bad foot.

While these must dance untrippingly, and words
Come tripping off their tongues in prose fandangos,
Reeling through open forms, their manifesto
A studious ignorance of pentameters.

Cursing their natural fathers, they eschew
Old, worn-out Shakespeare. Shit, Mercutio,
Take that. Die, dog. Choke on your own discharge.
These free-verse guys have pulled the chain on you.

These high and mighty let their regular thoughts
Spiral down toilet throats with you old, square ones.

Pumped with breath-pauses, growing round and free,
Inspired, they now take flight. Oh, watch them soar

Out of their windows, over the startled streets,
Loosed by their slack, thin lines, raised up by pals'
Cheers, jokes, and dogmas wafting from the mountain—
Like puffed-up windbags full of angry gas.

Blown Voices

The First Testament

Mezzo Cammin

Halfway through life, and what? Faint voices wafted
Across the wasteland baked and level and bare.
Whispering, tweedling sounds — of those too weak
In life, who slid, of those once monstrous, tamed
By death, rehearsing. "Travelers," I inquired,
"What business keeps you in this middle air?"

Bystanders

"We saw the poor, the elderly, the hungry,
Huddling on wasted and polluted tracts.
We saw a people torched out of their homes.
Strangers we saw, with faces like our own,
Melting down women and children in the streets.
Some danced in it, while others fell back gagging."

Sons of de Sade

"In life, the pain of others twanged and throbbed
In us, resounding downward to ignite
The nether organs. Seeing the ultimate pain
In those we tortured, wave on wave of shock,

The rankest pleasure, channeled through our veins.
The plucker of the keenest chords was pain."

Avenging Angels
"We were the messengers of righteousness
Perching on high. We made judgment seem
Swift and clean, through a telescopic sight.
We saw no blood and might have been in Funland
Blasting electric bullets, bombs, and missiles
At dots riding in jerks across the screen."

News Managers
"When people sought the truth we fed them facts:
Numbers of sorties, tonnage and names of bombs,
With human-interest stories sandwiched in.
We rocked them nicely, not too hard, never
Gave the impression that we really liked it.
Left out the blood and guts. Fouls up the game."

Psy War Team
"We printed up two hundred thousand games
Of *Vietcong Monopoly*, and passed them out
To villagers, to show them how much fun
Defection could be. Players, preferably
Hard-core Vietcong, would set their markers down
On North Vietnam, or Go, and roll the dice."

Native Farmers
"Faceless we worked the land, married, and fought.
We heard that peace would come if we would not
Offend our foes. We settled down. Peace came
With bulldozers and tractors. Over the land

Peace plunged its heavy tracks. Faceless we bowed.
And layer on layer we fertilized the crops."

Optimists
"We soaked their nests with gas and lit a match . . .
The plagues, the Indian wars, the Lisbon earthquake,
The ruins of London, Dresden, Nagasaki,
The Armenian massacres, the Jews in death camps
Whose one way out was through the chimneys, all
Mere anthills smoldering in the blaze of heaven."

Catastrophists
"A coarsening of spirit through knowledge? Yes:
Unspeakable machines break rumbling through
The nightmare, trucks with missiles. Built to fire,
Must they be fired? Why must they? Just because
In the day of night, in the eye of eyes, we saw
The cities of the world and they were burning."

The Country I Remember

I had a sister lovely in my sight. — Stickney

"Sister, where are you in these torrid wastes
   Through which I flutter, light as middle air,
   Half knowing where I go, still floundering
   In you, as if I were a puff of smoke
   Drawn by some distant duct or flue toward you.
   Mother and Father, bedded in their urn,
   Have made their vaporous exit. Here we are.
   O draw me forth and tell me without shame
   We are purified not dirtied by our flame.
   And take me in. Our tender shades will lighten,
   And each will glow in each, and be the same.
   Peace to our shades and let us live and burn."

"There was that story Father used to skip —
   How mother Earth once bore three slimy things
   With a hundred heads and hands. And father Heaven
   So hated them he buried them alive. So she
   Worked on her favorite son with wiles, till he,
   Gelding the father, took his power and throne.
   Grotesque. I felt it deep in me. Brother,
   Our love seemed horrible, for all ways led

To guilt and to the compensating will
To motherhood. Now, when I think of it,
I can't imagine why I balked at it,
Or why I shied and let us die alone."

"We set our shoulders to the tasks we chose:
One worked the family farm and one taught children
Drawing and writing in the Eastside slums.
Luther and Ellen were our names. What matter?
City and farm and work and world go by.
We glow in each as ghostly emanations
And light each other's lights as once we did,
Though now the feeling is like tingling music
Uninterrupted. Hovering not far off
From where we found ourselves and suffered it,
We go on living with our ancestors,
With some degree of individual self,

"Some dregs of sticky matter to burn off,
While year by year our spirits resolve themselves
Into the great fantasia. Still what joy
Is in our meeting and commingling, each
The other's perfect spark, withindoors keeping.
The match that scratched against the plaster wall
Ignites the room. Not just an afterlife,
Recipients of a second feeling life,
We rise coequal in the eye of heaven
Whose warmth awoke the fragrant earth we smelled
In spring before the popping out of flowers
On the back forty. There we scouted out

"Our willow island, where we played, until
The power project dammed the stream and sank it. . .

Our parents let us play and play we did—
Touched and untouched, at first, as children will,
Then touched more darkly, reaching further down,
Touching each other's chords until we sang.
Some nights we carried on between the rooms,
Moaning, half asleep and half awake,
Tossing our long black curls. The wind outside
Might stir the eaves and shutters, and the house
Might heave with longing in its very rafters
Before you came to me or I to you . . .

"'Shh, it's the wind, the night.' 'We shouldn't do it—
What if they caught us?' 'Shh.' 'Oh kiss me there.
And there. Don't stop. Don't ever stop it. Be
My nibbling rabbit.' 'Be my nibbling tigress.'
'Take what we can tonight and let the day
Know nothing of it. Now, again.' 'Again!'
Such joy we took in secret that our fears
Grew in proportion. Fear is sire of guilt
And social conscience. Springs that boil within
Premove us toward responsibilities.
Who could have told us of it? No one watched us.
Our parents may have had some glimmerings,

"But never ones to chastise us, they held
Their peace, and what was in us grew to be
A rapture. O dear sister, O dear brother—
O dear disaster favored from afar!
Father's books fed us. We were lord and lady.
The annual visit to the county fair
To us was like a trip to Rome, not just
Balloons and ferris wheel and cotton candy,
But bulls and slaves and victors in their cars.

It was Dido and Aeneas. In the attic,
Refinement of the savage held us most,
That book of Jews and Romans, Greeks and gods . . .

"It asked us if our love were fated, if
Something genetic ruled our trysts. It said:
Sweet reason, left to its devices, would
Weed out the bad from good, until we die.
Of madness and perversion it said nothing.
It sang the lore of mind and body, all
Indulgent of their use. It trained the will
To good, that reasonable lovers may
Attain, who therefore with impunity
May come to gazing, holding hands, and kissing,
Because of all chaste acts they most desire
By touching of the flesh to draw their spirits

"Out of the body, letting each with each
Commingle and by subsequent degrees
Pour themselves into one another's body . . .
Mother and Father, now so rarified,
Are so unburdened that they live in us
As much as in themselves. We hear them say,
'Only an age or so to take your joy
Before your spirits are blended in the vast
Swirl of the universal elements,
Sublimed away, at last made one, to be
Reborn in something altogether other.
Peace to our shades and let us live and burn.'"

Maced at Chartres

Beyond the porch a woman strummed and sang
Of dark Vietnams, of youth and land betrayed
By elders. Near her, on her tambourine,
Lay a few coins tossed down by passers-by.

Whatever it was, the dismal day, the tourists'
General insouciance — what can tourists see,
Who come with guides in sin-proof flocks to gawk
At flying buttresses and stained-glass saints?

Did she dislike the tourists? Did she think
That all were blinkered, deaf, impervious to
The prophecy? And had she planned a way
To drive the sting of her displeasure home? —

Whatever it was, while some were in the shop
Sipping canned soda, buying Chartres brochures,
And some were idling round the square, she pulled
Out of her cloak the cylinder, and sprayed.

What wind there was wafted the caustic cloud
Across the square and toward the shop. Eyes flowing,

Coughing and sneezing, people blindly ran
This way and that, leaving behind their drinks,

Umbrellas, souvenirs. Rude chaos. Then
The fuss was over. There was the shining bus,
The rolling fields of wheat, the friendly voice
Of the guide resounding in their ears, the tires

Droning along the mindless miles. Some chittered
And quipped and laughed like those who've never wept,
Discussing dinner plans, the next day's tour.
Reason prevailed. Some spoke of Chartres. Some slept.

Paris Again

As one who long years homesick for his town
Returns in hope of some light-hearted tune,

One hears a beggar croon a mournful rhyme
Of youth and innocence and love's old crime . . .

A song we knew by heart and then half lost.
And this is all? You ask, what is the cost?

Glad music? No, the songs we once admired
Are still being sung. For us they are acquired . . .

This is the burden of the song we sing.
O years, O weariness, O cost of being.

The Eye Egg

As blind potato eyes in darkness sprout, the eye
Hatched before the dawn of light, not knowing why.

What, if not touch, could give it such necessity
To force through darkness till the light was born to see?

Home was good, food was good, fed through the gut.
Space was seamless, warm, and humming. Time held. But

Touch thrust up, and opening length & breadth & height
Before it, moved among them in a field of light,

Till grits of seeds their cases burst, and flowers sprang,
And all their atoms, in the light of morning, sang:

"What though no mercy called us forth, no greater eye
Regards us or takes notice when we droop and die?

"We praise, with all our tingling particles and quarks,
Whatever programmed us and runs through us and works."

Lost Passenger

The tall grass lessens year on year
    Beneath an acid heaven.
The tree that held a hundred nests
    Forgets and is forgiven.

Now, in the radiant haze of summer,
    Unseal your ears and eyes
And hear the silence as a thousand
    Ghostly wings arise,

And see the fields of fallen bodies
    Blinking and half dead.
"God's creaters — a wicked wastey thing,"
    Leatherstocking said.

But year on year, with guns and clubs,
    Men slaughtered all they could.
The rains and snows of autumn came
    And washed out the blood.

Donald Petersen, born in Minneapolis, studied at Carleton College with Arthur Mizener, Reed Whittemore, and others; spent a year at the Sorbonne; and later at the Poetry Workshop of the University of Iowa, studied with Paul Engle, Robert Lowell, John Berryman, and Karl Shapiro. During two summers at the Indiana School of Letters he studied with John Crowe Ransom, Allen Tate, Randall Jarrell, and Delmore Schwartz. He taught at Iowa and is now professor emeritus at the State University of New York at Oneonta. His other published collection of poems is *The Spectral Boy*.

The New Criterion is recognized as one of the foremost contemporary venues for poetry with a regard for traditional meter and form. The magazine was thus an early leader in that poetic renaissance that has come to be called the New Formalism. Building upon its commitment to serious poetry, *The New Criterion* in 2000 established an annual prize, which carries an award of $3000. Donald Petersen is the first winner.